ALONG THE PEAL OF DRUMS

Collected Poems
1990-2015

AMBROSE MASSAQUOI

Sierra Leonean Writers Series

Along the Peal of Drums

ISBN: 978-99910-54-33-9

Sierra Leonean Writers Series

DEDICATION

For the pleasure of Maama:
Lover, on whose diamond heart
I have etched the dream songs I sing

In Memory of J.E.M. Blango:
Guardian, from whose buffalo head
I drank my first fill of conscious music

To the glory of God:
Maker, in whose Spirit-Word
I live and move and find my groove

TABLE OF CONTENTS

HERALD OF YELIBAS

Foreword by Joanna Skelt

Along the Peal of Drums is a startlingly alive array of poems rooted in the land and cultures of Sierra Leone and yet echoing concerns, disillusionments, and passions that speak universally. Sprinkled with a fair share of lustiness, this fecund and vital engagement with life drives Massaquoi's meandering and shape-shifting spirit through a range of different voices and themes: from an opening poem spreading out from night's thighs ("We Light Our Fires in the Village") to the channeled passion of the village depiction in "Nostalgia." This energy builds up in crescendo as Massaquoi booms out in praise -singing voice with warrior spirit in the spectacular poem "Bo of THEPEOPLE." In this, Massaquoi conjures a fiercely protective defense of Bo against rebel invasion, using the constant refrain "I am Bo." Multilayered and culturally embedded, this crafted piece speaks through the present, and historically, to reveal a city formed from clay, from spirit, from ancestors, from red earth and pure resistive will.

More than the usual emphasis on conflict in poems of this period, this is a close-up lived experience, with the old vying with and contradicting the new, which remains at the foreground of this collection. Woven throughout are themes of hardship and competition for money, corrupting relationships along the way. Massaquoi for instance describes a bus trip as "Just human beings/Hard/On each other" ("Bo by Bus"). Similarly, the indulgence of appetites by the rich and the realities of contemporary bar culture is revealed in "Sugar Daddy Dance":

Pounding away
All he is worth
In yellow babes
Younger than his kids

Influences of Cheney-Coker are evident in terms of freeness and experimentation with form and a tendency, occasionally, towards surreality. Massaquoi's best work, however, comprises concrete descriptions, insightful metaphor and channeled emotions.

Imbued with a palpable sense of urgency and a passion for writing, Massaquoi has emerged alongside other poets such as Gbanabom Hallowell and Farouk Sesay whose genesis was the Falui Poetry Society which emerged during the civil conflict. As such, *Along the Peal of Drums* comes at an important point in the resurgence of Sierra Leonean literature and is a welcome addition to the genre.

Dr. Joanna Skelt
University of Birmingham, UK
City of Birmingham Poet Laureate, 2013-2014
14 October, 2015

Introduction by Mohamed Gibril Sesay

Ambrose Massaquoi is a poet of/after/about fulfilment in love, dance and music, about their uplifting and seamier sides, and the grey areas in-between, and about how our search for love, dance and music is sometimes corrupted both in intent and action. Our tragedy is that what should uplift oftentimes debases us, what should bring joy we twist onto bringing pain.

Love is God's gift to us, but Ambrose mulls the desolation that the absence of a finer sense of God brings into our pursuit of the good life. He does not say this in an in-your-face way per se. We however are able to tease out these concerns through the prisms of what we know about his life—he being a churchman, a lover of music, a player of instruments, and known amongst us during our cutting-teeth days at the Falui Poetry Society for fidelity to the love of his life: his wife, Bridget. Thus even in those toddler days, we saw his poems as well-crafted laments about the sometimes inverted life we live and won't leave. It is as if he softly says to us, "For want of fidelity, the people perish."

So, a central motif in *Along the Peal of Drums* is this concern about the worship of the underbelly of a trinity of sex, dance and song, and our genuflection before the craven images of our lust. Here, Ambrose lays bare the heavy burden of flesh on noosed necks of souls weakened by lack of nourishment from moral trainers, some of whom feed on the very flesh of those seeking liberation from the burdens of too much corporeality— "holyman the pro/dripping holywater under sweat of estrus/...with semen of/sharks seething in his prescriptions."

But one also sees defiance in the face of this plague of "goat onslaught" on our loins, and if one may add, lions. I like this, of loins and lions. Loins humbling lions; crotches on crutches after the assaults. The poet himself finds love, true-true love as we say in

Sierra Leone, after journeying with crotches on crutches. He finds wholesomeness in the love of his life ("the streams of love/to clean my slate"), and victory in the Cross ("In my crotch I carry the Cross"). Looking back, however, Ambrose sees too many yet on crutches, too many yet eating "set-ripe" bananas. Perhaps this is what gives him the passion and compassion to write such beautiful poetry—an artist who has gone through hades, and survived onto an Easter of Love, sending rope-ladders of enlightened verse to rescue former comrades trapped in the oubliettes of "He-Goat-I-ism."

Ambrose's oeuvre is also a commentary on the socio-politics of our own type of mess—of fratricidal rebels during our war, of rogue politicians, of "detonated rice-bags of/Promises on the citizenry," of "battle cries of a revolution that/Revolves on its name/Only." Most times, however, we see this commentary through micro-descriptions of the relationships between man and woman, and the relationship each individual has with his/her loins or manhood or womanhood. We see oppression in how men treat women, we see mutual exploitation between sugar daddies/mommies and sugar babies.

Extensively, Ambrose writes about individuals negotiating their destinies through thickets of national hopes and obstacles—willing the toss of rain and sun, the toss of the coin of their circumstance to show the heads or tails they had bet on. But lo, many find oppression in the sun, sycophancy in the moon, loss in lust, and "spit disgust" at the "damned rain."

Again, there is recurring resistance to the debasement, not only at the personal man-woman level, but also at the macro level—a religio-sociology of resistance. We see this in the poem "Sung for Jonah," where we find the line "Peal of Drums" that is the title for this collection. This poem celebrates one man's resistance against forces who would not hearken to the people's voice. But that man's voice, a singularity of the people's voice, is the "seaside stone that breaks the backbone of waves," the "knee-bone of elephant that damages the hyena's teeth." This theme of resistance is also seen in the Poem, "Bo of the People." I remember this poem, and others like "Titi Bum Boat", "Definition," "Donkey Blues"... how Ambrose used to read them to us during our crèche days as poets, when we rub-skinned against one another for poetic warmth in the bitter cold of a war that a mindless corporal had baled upon us.

Several of these poems name the villains and heroes of our national efforts. Heroes: Jonah, Zainab, Kendenka. Villain: Foday Sankoh, leader of the fratricidal rebels in Sierra Leone's civil war. Our poet also brings into view the orbit of friends: Gbanabom Hallowell (on the joy of gathering poet-friends), Moses Kainwo (on the pranks and dance of friendship, Khadi Mansaray (on struggles with illness), Ben Ecklu (on the pain of death). Indeed, Ambrose is in many measures a poet of the personal concrete moment rather than of the abstract and general. His insights are suffused with details of specific occasions in his life: of being sleepless in America, of travelling to the city of his boyhood—Bo, of overlooking Freetown from his hilly home at New England Ville, of being in Pepper Clarke's hilly Ibadan, and also of persons he encounters such as neighbors, vendors, and taxi drivers. He anchors his metaphors in the details of these encounters. It is not about abstract ideas dominating his renditions; rather it is the other way round. He presents concrete encounters about rain and sun, "boys and girls naked as peeled potatoes /plunging into the pulse of August rain and not ashamed," "cobra smoked out of his hold" and "full blown faces of petals." These are all specifics about particular moments that roll the drums for us to join him in his dance "on sheaves on our threshing floors/and measure our laughter in bushels."

Mohamed Gibril Sesay
Author, *This Side of Nothingness; At the Gathering of Roads*
29 April, 2016

Commentary by Sheikh Umarr Kamarah

For many years since independence, literary production in Sierra Leone lagged behind other countries in the West African region. But in the past three decades, Sierra Leonean literature has witnessed a significant boom never before experienced. The existence of Sierra Leonean publishing houses like the Sierra Leone Writers Series has been a boon to that boom. In particular, poetry has flourished in the country and Sierra Leonean poets both within and without the country have been steadily producing collections of poetry. A new and impressive cadre of poets has appeared on the scene, and has been steadily growing both in number and quality of production. Ambrose Massaquoi is part of that impressive cadre of Sierra Leonean poets. Although *Along the Peal of Drums* is his debut collection, Massaquoi is an established voice across the landscape of Sierra Leonean Poetry, having extensively published in both local and international journals and anthologies since the early 90s. Also, in 1994, he became the third Sierra Leonean, after Yulisa Amadu Maddy and Syl Cheney-Coker, to represent the country in Iowa University's International Writing Program. Thus, this is an entrance by a poet of considerable stature.

The collection honors a diversity of themes of contemporary interest, and does not lend itself to easy splicing. But the arrangement of the poems affords the reader leitmotifs of the collection by means of its categorization into three major sections: **Luv-a-Dubs and All that Jazz, Sundance,** and **Beats in Penumbra**. Themes such as creativity, a life close to nature, love, hustle, pain, resilience, hope, and many more, are explored in this debut collection. In spite of this diversity, each section is dominated by a particular theme or set of themes.

The title of the collection, *Along the Peal of Drums*, is very apt as it captures the thread that holds the diverse themes together even as they are scattered across the wide canvas the collection covers. The phrase, "peal of drums," among other things, draws attention to the musical notes and language of the drum which form an integral part of the festival of poetic creation in the African culture. The poem is not meant to be written, but to be sung; and the drum is always present in the drama of poetic creation. The title thus serves as a window to the poet's conceptualization of the process of poetic creation.

The first section of the collection is dominated by the themes of love, creation, and creativity dramatized in different poems and in different ways. The collection opens with a poem titled, "Pastime with a Poem," which captures the creative process by which a poem comes to be "born." Massaquoi is the only Sierra Leonean poet I have read who begins his collection with a poem dealing with the process of poetic creation. The process is presented as some sort of flirtatious affair in which a spark of poetic inspiration teases the poet, tickles his "mind" and pinches his "brain." The creative "thought" is spoken of as a lighthearted lady who comes to the poet and pulls his legs, makes him "tumble," sending him "into blackout." Then suddenly, "like rain in September," she falls on the poet from above, surprising him with the contents and shape of the poem. The poet can now put on paper that which has taken shape in the Mind. In the poetic creation, as in any other literary creation, the imagination is privileged.

Massaquoi exhibits an ability to infuse a theme with potent metaphors and captivating imagery. This ability is shown throughout the collection, as exemplified by the poem "We Light Our Fires in the Village." In this poem, Massaquoi deals with night life in a village. Here, "village" evokes not only simplicity of life, but also closeness to nature. The absence of electricity and other so-called modern amenities makes "Night" a dark and mysterious moment in the village. But Massaquoi presents life in the village in a different light. In this village, "Fires" take the place of electricity and provides warmth and light at the same time. Story-telling sessions are held

"Between the thighs of Night." The use of the metaphor, "thighs of Night" triggers the captivating anatomical imagery ascribing limbs to an element of Nature. Village night life is characterized by stories, which embody the history and epistemological framework of the village; songs (poems), which embody the literary/cultural production of the village; and dance, which embody the entertainment dimension. "Between the thighs of Night" refers the sensual and temporal square in which village is celebrated. This is a poem where the stars, the moon, the fires, the Harmattan, and the drums conspire to create a life close to Nature and to enhance the production of literature, a theme started in the first poem. Metaphors such as, "…tongues of fire," "the womb of Night," "glossolalia of jungle Drums" are fresh and unforced, and therefore potent.

The first section has many more of such evocative poems including "The plague advances," a poem dedicated to Syl Cheney-Coker, Sierra Leone's most celebrated poet and novelist. Also here are the "Bum Boat" poems and "Gambe River Gal" which hint at the insidious socio-political problems that result from decadent living.

Then there is "Onan: The First Romance," a poem alluding to Biblical tradition. The poem, in my view, is about an aborted attempt at procreation. Onan is said to be an insignificant character in the Bible—younger brother of Er and son of Judah. When Er died without an offspring, Onan was required to impregnate his wife, Tamar, so that the first-born son of that union would carry on the name of the deceased man. But when the moment came, Onan "wasted his seed on the ground." It is this Biblical story that Massaquoi adapts into a beautifully crafted work of art through the use of authentic and familiar African objects or items:

> The night throbs/With goat songs
> The raw sangba/Smell splits his pa-
> Late like bad palm oil

But at what is called moment supreme,

> Spurts of milk dust/Shooting-stars shoot
> Across the dark room/Future Fruits flung
> As wild-grass seeds/To kiss cold concrete.

The title of the second section, **Sundance**, is intriguing. Sundance has been defined as, "A dance performed by North American Plains Indians in honor of the Sun and to prove bravery by overcoming pain." Although this section houses a diversity of themes including tributes to people like James Jonah, Zainab Bangura, and a poem dedicated to another poet, Gbanabom Hallowell, the dominant theme is that of resilience in the teeth of pain and suffering. The Sun is the dominant metaphor. This Sun—in the context of APC, the war, pain, and suffering—can be seen as life-denying, although it is generally regarded as a source of life.

In the first poem of the section, "Sung for Jonah," the poet showers James Jonah with praises for his role in the fight to bring back Democracy to the poet's country of Sierra Leone. In fact, the title of the entire collection comes from a line in this poem. Jonah is presented as a voice that vibrates the "Tongue of the Town tom-tom" ...a voice that "breaks the backbone of waves." Clearly, the poet reveres James Jonah and declares him the voice from God. His is a voice derived "from the testicles/Of timeless oracles," and one that "collects a country/To reclaim the/Footprints of its future."

In a three-stanza poem titled, "Mammy Musu Salutes Sun," a woman pleads with the Sun in the morning, afternoon, and evening for "palm-oil," "fireside rainbow," and "a mat to sleep on," respectively. The poem "Solar songs" continues this exploitation of the metaphor of the Sun. Here, peasants sweat under the Sun to sing songs that only create Icons that oppress them:

The songs/They sang

The man/The toe/The toehold
All sinewed in their throats
…
Too tough to swallow/Or spit out.

In "New Dawn," the shape of the poem draws attention to itself. The poet uses the technique of ostranenie here by presenting the poem in a strange way in order to enhance its perception. The poem is shaped like a bowl made of three stanzas of 3-3-2 lines. In the poem, much like William Butler Yeats in "The Second Coming," the poet warns of something on the horizon that looks like the past.

In "Knock Iron Soja," the poet talks about how Foday Sankoh, the founder and Leader of the Revolutionary United Front (RUF), "bails war/To Pujehun," from where the fire consumed the entire country. And in "Bo of THEPEOPLE," a tribute is paid to the people of Bo for their solid will to protect and defend their town. Bo is the speaker in the poem:

I am Bo
The potter's Clay/crafted to cradle
The prototype of/The people's indomitability
…
I am Bo
The tiger roar of Poro
Giving birth to/The people's power in a/Sacred bush.

In "For Zainab Bangura," the poet once again pays tribute to one of the female voices of Sierra Leone that helped bring democracy to the country. Like Jonah, Zainab is said to have: "ascended the/Sky of valiant flames to/Birth us one deathless moment."

In "Grassroots Poet," a thank you note is written to Gbanabom Hallowell for having created the space for the creative impulse in the poet to be fully exploited. In the poem poetry or the creative impulse

17

is celebrated as the purging of emotions; a creative orgasm that calms secular nerves and maims unbridled anxieties:

> I am Falui/One armed combustive poet
> Twin brother of elephant grass
> …
> I who once stabbed my heart/with torments for my Sierra
> Shattered my grit on her/Peaks of pain.

Falui provides the channel to handle the torments and pain of the poet's environment.

The final section, **Beats in Penumbra,** is dominated by the themes of reflection and hope. The section opens with a poem called, "Definition," which defines poets and, by extension, all creative artists in a country like Sierra Leone. The four lines of this poem, pasted from the top to the bottom of the page, leaving among them empty spaces, draw attention to the poem, and the perception of poets. Here, again, Massaquoi demonstrates his mastery of ostranenie, a technique ingenious writers like him successfully use to heighten sense perceptions.

In "Nostalgia," the poet yearns for days of yesteryears when the "music of the rice mortars of harvest days" were not mute, and "weaverbirds choral" in palm trees were alive. Alas, those days are no more. "Invocation" is a prayer for agricultural fecundity; a prayer for a future without hunger. It is a prayer to Mother Earth, to "Heave to the dreams" of the people and open up "when our seeds" penetrate her body. A prayer for Mother Earth to "Yield us dances on sheaves on our threshing floors/And measure our laughter in bushels." This is a poem of hope for joy and happiness. The poet, in this poem moves from the personal pronoun to the collective pronoun "we" and its objective counterpart, "ours." The idea of production is couched in the agricultural metaphors and imagery in the poem

18

In Epitaph, Massaquoi remembers his son who died at birth. It is an intensely personal poem:

Your face/From the long distance
Of elephant's memory
Your face/Lazarus come forth/Smack out of my loins

In "For Khadi," the poet sends a bouquet of encouragement to a friend, sister, and colleague poet who's is struck by a stroke. The poet celebrates Khadi's strength, resolve, resilience, and character. He refers to her as, "soul sister of the fertile/Long-lived Nile" who can never be shaken by gossips and back stabs.

In "Ubuntu," Massaquoi returns to the communal theme. Ubuntu is a Bantu (African) philosophy which means, "Humanity toward others." It is based on the idea that one is only human because of society. Contrary to Rene Descartes' Western Philosophy of *Cogito ergo sum* (I think, therefore I am) which privileges the Individual over the Community, in Ubuntu Philosophy, the community is privileged over the individual. So, it is "We are, therefore I am." In this Ubuntu philosophy, "nONE is/Good enough to be aLONE… nONE is/God enough to be I AM."

Ambrose Masaquoi ends his collection with a poem of joy, music, song, and dance. It is a song of hope for the return of happiness and the flourishing of the creative impulse in Sierra Leone:

Out of the bull's/Eye of the bush
Buffalo's heart/Land, drum/Beats burst
…
Breaks/Out of our bone/Marrows with
One cracking carnival
Across the country.

The collection ends on a positive note and recommends a philosophy of communal responsibility and the abandoning of selfishness in the struggle for a better society.

Ambrose Massaquoi is by all standards an accomplished poet. His knack to employ fresh and potent metaphors and similes, on which the imagery of his poetry rides, is one of his powerful assets. Much like Farouk Sesay and Ahmed Koroma, he uses familiar and accessible language to convey a profound message. A fascinating distinctiveness of his as a writer is his tendency to use humor to convey his message, as seen in a number of the poems here. This collection is a masterful work of art which everyone will enjoy reading.

Dr. Sheikh Umarr Kamarah
Professor and Chair
Language and Literature
Virginia State University
March 9, 2016

LUV-A-DUBS & ALL THAT JAZZ

Pastime with a Poem

My mind
Kicks with
Antics
There is a
Thought
Tickling me
There

She pinches
My brain
I turn
She ducks
Pulls my legs
And I tumble
Into blackout

She lights up
Right there
Fullmoon ripe
In the dark
Of my skull
Seesawing like
Seaweed on
Ocean tide

Swelling
Shrinking
Swaying from
Side to side

I dash
Stretch and grab…
Surf bubbles

Sing saucy
Songs in the
Hollow of my head

My brain is
Hauled into
Despair
Suspended between
Words
Sounds
Wriggling for power

Then from above
Like rain
In September
She falls all
Over me and
Floods me with
Fantasia
Figures
Vocabulary
Vivacity

I grab my pen
"This time I gotcha!"
There is light laughter
And she's spread
Into a poem
On wastepaper

We Light Our Fires in the Village

Between the thighs of
Night

There are stories
There are songs
There's rhythm & dance

Glossolalia of jungle
Drums that urge us
Round tongues of fire

The ardent moon comes
To tease shadows on
Mudhouse walls

The stars too
Fireflies in bloom
To nibble nipples of girls playing coocoo

There's hint in the
Hip-swing of light
Harmattan breeze

Toward which we turn
Like palm trees
On the crest of waves

Then catch our dreams
Before the fire expires
Before we vanish to sleep

Like those shadows on
Mudhouse walls
Into the womb of

Night

Onan: The First Romance

The night throbs
With goat songs

The raw sangba
Smell splits his pa-
Late like bad palm-oil

A yellow moon
Comes cantering
Across the courtyard

Slips between bed
Sheets; her feline
Face pulsating on

His primed pelvis
Honey snaking
His bottom-belly

The yellow urge
Pokes the white heat
Along his wild spine

Alas O Lord!
Alas O Lord!
Man is overwhelmed

His sweaty palm
Strokes the poker
Working hot dances

Spurts of milk dust
Shooting-stars shoot
Across the dark room

Future fruits flung
As wild-grass seeds
To kiss cold concrete

How he rouses
From moonmating
With his own shadow

His goat beard
Stained with guilt

Titi Bum Boat

Titi Bum Boat, Titi Bum Boat
Aboard a boat to grease a Goat
Bouncing her big bums up & down
God knows what she will bring to town

Titi Bum Boat, Titi Bum Boat
On board the boat oils V.D. Goat
Then hurries home baroque and bloat
With God knows what under her coat

28

Titi Bum Boat Is a Towel

Titi Bum Boat
Is a towel
Tied around the
Loins of tycoons

Titi Bum Boat
Is a towel
Is a cow tied
To the phalli
Of the fertile

Titi Bum Boat
Is as towel
As a campaign
Into which politicians
Pour sweat from
Brows of their people

Titi Bum Boat
Is a towel
Sodden with our sweat

Fat as a cow
On the toil of the land

Yet, still open
As a ballot box
To the balls of power

Mammy Queen

Face florid as her
Waxed African prints

Eyes wildflowers
Like those lovers
She grows undercover

She's got pots of gold
In her hearings
Neck deep into pearls

Her lips sipping glass all the time
Her lips speaking class all the time

Gambe River Gal

Gambe River gal
She want sheen like silk
Gambe River gal
She want white like milk

Tourist rush dey on
She shine shine as silk
Tourist rush done done
She charred white as milk

Inversions for a Boogie Woman

From toot to toot
The picked-up lass
Rode the life of her dreams

From band to band
The drum 'n' bass
Swayed the hips of her dance

From door to door
The high-heeled sass
Clicked her walk into shops

Boogie woogie from Paris to Macau
Boogie woogie across the bridge & now...

From foot to foot
The trampled grass
Blades of her stifled screams

From hand to hand
The rumpled pass
Piece of beat-up romance

From floor to floor
The shattered glass
Of chichi smiles and Schnapps

Love on the Rocks

The chemistry of her creamface
The psychedelia of her
Purple blouse
Galvanized toenails
Trinkets and
Things
The self-assured control
Of her geometry
Tugged hard at his heart

Simple soul
Like a tactless tongue
His heart skipped
Brisk
Missed
Slipped on the polished pavement
Between her postured breasts
And fell full length in love

Legs & Dreams

She belongs to
Beaches
Blue skies
Bottles and
Ballrooms

Big Sissy
Substantial with
Lightlife
(light laughter
light legs
et cetera)
Looking for child

He is typical
Green with
Pimples and
Dimples

An upstart who
Spends his days
In day dreams
And night dreams
With a pungent
Passion for
Delicacies like
Goat liver
Garnished clams
Et cetera
Looking for bigtime

It is only a
Matter of time

Only a matter
Of life and dreams
Before they meet
At a table
In a bar

Delicately He drums
His dreams
To her
Chewing on his
Goat liver
All the while

She listens lightly
Laughing lightly
Leaning lightly
Living lightly
Within his dreams
Making them her own for a while

What happens next
Behind the bar
In a night
Neatly knit
Is your guess

Light Legs clams
Around the Goat
Delicate Dreams
Drools in the Ballroom

After all is said
Spent and done
They part

She empty
With his dreams

He pregnant with the
Refuse of her light legs

Mourning Marley

In the dancehall—
Logwood burning in a night
Pregnant with foofooballs of blackout—
Flames of our dances leap along
The raw sounds of
Roots
Rock
Reggae

We jamming…
Surge upon urge
Gush upon rush of rude boys
Lush with psychedelic
Layers of sweat and
With heads locked like dreads
In puffs of pot

Dem sisters jamming too…
Some in china wigs
Some in natty braids
Some splotched by bleaches
Others stretched out like fresh perm
In skintight skirts and tubes

Soul rebels we all
Kinky in the heat of the jam

Lips lisp to lips
Arms arouse arms
Legs unlatch legs
In this steel pulse of passions
That rise along the
Pan sound of Barrett's drumming

Every now and again our
Tongues catch the fire
Flick to lick froths of ecstasy
Which wink from
Bickering beer bottles
While our legend waits in vain
Under the lambent lights
To satisfy our souls

Sugar Daddy Dance

His wife is a dancer
She dances the foxtrot
He is tired of trotting
In the same foxhole

Sweet Sixteen dances too
She does Lucky Dube tunes
He wants to get lucky with
A sweet teen to skank him
Sixteen on a dancefloor

Friday he gets lucky with
Sweet Sixteen off school
Dressed in purple and blue
Skin baby smooth
Mellow yellow like
Summer Country butter

Saturday he escapes the Fox
Through the backdoor
Drives his yellow babe
In a baby Benz
To Bintumani

At Bintumani
In a room full of
Bulls and Bums
Boozing froth and stuff
Bouncing like balls
To rub-a-dubs
Her hips are a steady drag
Reggae bass
Dragging him to the dancefloor

Her hips her skins pounding
Reggae drums
Pounding his ribs on the dancefloor

Her hips are knife-edge
Reggae rhythms
Knifing his loins on the dancefloor

The dance fills his loins
Goes to his head
Down his spine
Into his nerves
Through his entire system

Like a Rasta
Soaked in marijuana
Possessed with the
Philosophy of his prophet
He drones on the dancefloor
His dread goatee
Glistening with slobber
On the dancefloor

The first piece ends
The dance suspends
Another piece
Shall we dance please

The skank begins
To get strong
The skank turns
Into a Limba dance
A strongstrong dance
A strongstrong rope
Around his life

Dragging him from the foxhole
Dragging him from the Fox
Dragging him from that
Brood of foxy children
He fails to pay fees for

Our man is strong in
The dance now
Limbaman strong
Pestle strong
Pounding his life
In blooming mortars
Pounding away
All he is worth
Like Spider
In the mortars of his lust—

His time
His money
His strength
His soul
His name
His work
All he is worth
In yellow babes
Younger than his kids
By the Fox
For a daily dance

Each time a piece ends
The dance suspends
Leaving our man suspended
Like an end of a dance
Between home and more

The Plague Advances
(for Syl Cheney-Coker)

women who have drunk bucketsful of water
now stampede the atlantic for their holyman the pro
phet their illuminati
desperation barking through the stonewalls of their gonads
desert discharging ordure to the point of
delirium in their chronic chancres

from the ocean floor to meet them
at the point of their plague
he comes forth
their holyman
the pro
dripping holywater under sweat of estrus
luminous from bermuda's triangle with semen of
sharks seething in his prescriptions

each woman offers redredwine for his meditation
each offers 1 bagrice 1 drumoil 1 piececloth for his inspiration
and from fetishes of raweggs and redcloth
he makes his monolithic blacksoap
emerge from under his redfrock

seamen stare as women who have drunk bucketsful scoop his
semen in buckets to burgeon the monumental ghost stones
of their catacombs
of their tombs
of their wombs

and their holypro
their bodhisattva
chanting abracadabra

steams off in ecstasy
to make his yang ubiquitous on atlantis

now from the hydrotherapy
o Cheney my soothsayer
throbbing to the rhythm and blues of
seawaterful of sharks in their chancres
o Cheney they stream back
women who have drunk bucketsful of water
stream back to sleep with men who have died of gangrene

Casanova

Still goes the gallant
Stronger than March sun
Wild with Billy's horns
Tangled in his pants
His goat beard feverish
Like a witchhunter

Still goes the gallant
Consternating the
Constellations with
The same small bagful
Of bubbles; with the
Same cloud of clichés

Still he goes, gallant
Electric among
The hoodwinkables
Goat's gloat in his eyes
Shocking their she-shells
In shady places

Still he'll go, gallant
Chasing those that chase
Plus those that are chased
An angel of death
Flaunting his magic
Burning but not burnt

Bastard Heritage

Do not listen to Billy Goatson
Do not stand your ears to
His sputtering
Wet-words
His mouth stinks
With the stench
Of his father's lust

It was only yesterday
I caught the bearded mistake
By a church gate
Spitting his father's faith
Into one abandoned soul
13 years old

The seed he sowed
With ease in her ears
Will soon set in the womb
To be damned, dumped, or denied

One more beguiled child
May soon drop out
Into this Abaddon
Called world
With a scandal to
Her record

And the shaggy
Son of the beast
Will go on
Sowing his father's filth
Bastardizing our universe

Dare the Devil

The ghost of
Goat crucified
Roams our rooms
Seeking a groin
To devastate

Let come the bull
I fear no goat
True or ghost
I am butt-proof

In my crotch
I carry the Cross
Three silver nails
Six inches each

I will catch
That ghost of Goat
By the horns
Spike the dirty old
Spook too

Sarah

Swills the smoke of her dying
Holds herself out like a burnt stick
To the mad hands of her bushman

Fifteen years her life's been on fire
Fifteen years belittled & bruised
Fifteen years battered & broken into
Face flat for his heels

There is the blood in her mouth
She'd love to spit into his
Animal face

But our man's world
Long ago burnt her liver
For such daylight witchcraft

So Sarah swigs the smoke of her fury
Crosses her heart before the terror of
Her caveman's lightning strikes

The last ember of her will to breathe
Smoldering in the ashes of her liver

Your Love Scares Me

(M, for Joe)

Your love scares
Me like a
Bleeding moon

Your love is a
Savage spirit
Ravishing the moon

Within the clutch
Of your male cult
Under the pressure
Of your manpower

I awake to my
Womanhood
& venture

To beg for
RE-COG-NI-TION!

Sexual Egotism Repulsed

When you come to me
Do not come to mount me
Do not come to ride me
As some Arab slaver
Would his beast of burden

Love me as life
I am your wife

Numb me not in
Some forest stream
Nip me not with
Sour leaves
To clip my
Womanhood with your
He-Goat-I-ism

Let our souls mesh
We are one flesh

No Beautiful Woman

Sticker in a taxi
NO BEAUTIFUL WOMAN
STAYS WITH ONE MAN
Black bold on rainbow

I shift the ideology
Like tiles in Scrabble
On the rack of my brain
Trying to spell SENSE
On the dashboard

I spell and check into
The lexicon of truth
The word is a winnow
With windows in it

I retrieve my tiles
And note FALLACY
In the files

Coconut Seeds of Love

Left fingers
Light as milkweed
Curve over
Strings of love

Right hand strikes
BM7 chord
Pitches tunes
New as thin
Slice of pumpkin in the sky

Dimensions to be cast
Upon the seas
Of the heart
Coconut seeds of
Love

A History of Love
(For Bridget)

It was in childhood we first yearned
The dew of dawn was fresh on fleece
Eden's earth still palm-butter soft
Breast water still smelled on our breaths
When we licked the sides of our hearts

Legend holds it was our debut
Into school. Our hands were ringed and
We were charged to help each other
Preserve the pinch of pleasure we
Both had; help ourselves cross the road

On the road, at the four-road where
Choice meets mind, I chose to straggle
Lay siege, deceive and be deceived
I, gecko, tried all sorts till I
 Tasted a monarch butterfly

Vanity of vanities, cried
Solomon. Let the libertine
Fly freely, fall on every chick
He is unfulfilled until he
Returns home to his missing rib

Eventually I came home
I ebbed from the gulf to nowhere
My Self torn, clipped down to size
Covered with the dust I had raised
I could not survive my own game

You were there, waiting and ready
With streams of love to clean my slate
With your fire to burn my files
With the wind to give me new life
And I was purged; and I was forged

On the altar of heart. Then
You breathed into me affection
That breathes like the Gola forest
Full of life like a fallen log
Like a rainbow spread before God

Until I willed to be born again
Into your life, yearn for you as
A child, cling to that ring of a
Helpmate, cherish that divine charge
I never really would have loved

Love Is an Issue

Love is an issue
To be learned
A living cell that
Will grow up to be
Misunderstood

One day you will
Wake up to it
An easy wall
A fragile thing
You stammer to touch

Other times a complex
Weave of web
A bamboo jungle
Before which you stand
Scratching scalp
Peering into your head
For answers

Sometimes
Periodic henna
Tears of unfulfilled egg
Running down your dis-
Appointed shins

Then up the passage of life
You feel its flagellations
You feel it fill your
Bosom with its
Breath, blood, bones
It's very life

54

Feeling like fingers
Thrust down your throat
A feeling
To throw
To hate
To cherish
And to keep
That which demands to
Suck and to suckle
Till it comes of age

Love is an issue
To be learned
An ant etherized
Whose entrails we
Must take care to
Examine or else
Butcher on the
Operating table

July12th: What Is My Song

Freetown
That night rained morning
Like a desert shower
Daisies bloomed, poppies bloomed

My song was a palm-bud
Singing love songs
Metered with laughter

Accra
Rains grow into a
Male pawpaw plant pregnant
With dreams: Futility!

My song is a palm tree
Still singing love
Songs undisturbed

Heartstorm

The flesh is
Fireplace
Sleeping
Dreaming
Strange fires

So cloud thick
O tempest of
My insides
Pulse with your fire
Gather your jaws and
Spit your spell
Into my eyes
That I may go
Blind to all else
But you

Strike
Bolt down
Hit my chest
Let me
Scratch
Cough
Stutter and be
Tuned off to all else
But you

On Setripe Sex

Peers pressure us
To eat our
Bananas setripe

They say it's nice
It is normal
Everybody's doing it

But let them souse
Bananas that cannot
Peel into salt water

Let them baptize
Bananas with
Umbilical cords
Still uncut
In carbide

Let them
O let them soften
Bananas of their love
Over latrines of the fast times

We will sit here
You and I
In this shade
Of patience
Counting sunsets
And raindrops
Till the bananas
Of our love
Split their skins
Open on the tree

Poison

Poison is not
Kill-chinch-kill-arata
Sure death on fishhead
Or dry bread
Under bed
Behind cupboard

Poison is not
Aversions we
STORE IN A SAFE PLACE
OUT OF REACH OF CHILDREN
Out of reach of our lives

Poison is perfume
Bottle of pure
Paradise poised
On my wife's
Dressing table

Poison is perfume
Plush scent of her presence
Pressing me out of breath
To the subtle apple
Of her supple neck

Poison takes my breath away...

Awaking Just Before Dawn

My bathroom brings itself
To the edge of a candle flame
& my eyes catch

Chimera of a shadow
Stripping on all
Four walls

& again my eyes catch
A quartermoon in the
Water closet

Towels, panties & other wet names
Loll like jumbo bats still
Asleep along its aura

Night stands in the shower
Washing down for the day
& when the last cock crows

Disappears in the body of my wife
Leaving a faded nightslip
On the bathroom floor

SUNDANCE

Sung for Jonah

Voice vibrating the
Tongue of the
Town tom-tom

Voice vibrating in the
Tunnel of the
Town crier's tongue

Voice—image of seaside
Stone that breaks the
Backbones of waves

Kneebone of elephant
That damages
Hyena's teeth

Voice of a prophet
Voice of the people
Voice from God who speaks

& knife cuts

Cutting across steeps
Along the peal of drums
To distant villages

Collecting a country
To reclaim the
Footprints of its future

Its present
Its past
Its eternity

Voice of a prophet
From the testicles
Of timeless oracles

Yielding to
The people the
Voice of God

I Now Blow

I now blow my own trombone
Croon on my own saxophone
Snap a piece of bone

From the ribs of my own
Poems... form, fettle and hone
It for one perfect tenor and tone

Stand alone atop Salone
& through my very own baritone
Blow the Sun my bit of cyclone

Mammy Musu Salutes Sun

Good morning Sun
Ow de breakfast show?
Please break my sleep
Into palm-oil today
Before you go go

Good afternoon Sun
Ow de revolution de go?
Please paint my fireside
Into rainbow today
Before you go go

Good evening Sun
Ow de go de go
Please spread my sleep
On a mat today
Before you go go

Solar Songs

(On The Making of Icons)

The solar songs
Peasants sang
Spliced the man
Toughened his
Toehold

The toehold
Dug deeper
Rooted rapidly
On their sweat

The songs
They sang
The man
The toe
The toehold
All sinewed in their throats

Became strong
As death
Sharp
As sting
Rough
As cough

Too tough to swallow
Or spit out

A Tink Say San Do Dem

At the inception of Sun
Infinitude rounds of
Witchgun-barreled speeches
Detonated ricebags of
Promises on the citizenry

3 days after
Third estate casualties
Coughed up regrets and fainted
Late into overpriced mass graves

Relentless
Sun struck the carnage on the
7th day with bayonets
(tipped with their very
Soles, palms, ripped private parts)
And transmuted them into zombies
With Okomfo Anokye's sword
Run through their tongues

40th day
No use now
O palmwine
O palmoil
O kolanut

Eternally now
They roam the rot of their underworld
With weed-seeds of shegita
Fecund on their resolve

En You Ge De Voice

(Dedicated to Dora – an infant grocer)

a ge de peppe a ge de sol a ge de yabas a ge de sweet sugar. . .!

To your voice
The junkseller's bell
In your throat
Hollering Bigmarket
On your head
Relations fasten for survival

Papa
The slave-driver's claw
In your blood
Still shadows spiders
On the edge of a broom
40 years in the civil service
And a crop of cobwebs
In dreams condemned
To show for it

Mama
The slave
Stranded in a fallopian imbroglio
Has cranked out a football team at 28
Now her dreams stay home
To wipe the diarrhea
Of a life ventricose
With malnutrition

And you…

You pitch your voice
The pitchfork of a
Hopeless labor
Restless in your throat
To seduce Sun to
Toss you a dream in their favor

a ge de peppe a ge de sol a ge de yabas a ge de sweet sugar. . .!

En you ge de voice

Freetown from New England Ville

Lions hunch from the east, stretch as
Crocodiles through my country's turtle-tail
Toward Sun's wash-yard; then swerve to
Gobble a city spat like kola-chaff spat to Sun's spleen
Facing it with a
Genie whose jaws run deeper than the rectum of River Rokel

April Fool's Poem

March 29th
Amid ragged sutra of
Rapel fretwork
I locate and lift my hand
Into cassava leaf
Across Garrison Street
To my friend, the poet, the
Reverend Moses Kainwo
His devout spectacles go past me to the
Concretion of heat and humidity
Which he holds
As if smoke
To his brain cells for critique
Perspiration down his shanks dribble the analysis across to me

    The Sun's energy is most
    Merciless in March

Yes, to the Ga of Ghana
This month denotes
Inside fire

    Especially so, now
    On my laid-off beard
    It is plait on top of lice
    A cephalo-pelvic disproportion in these
    Battle cries of a revolution that
    Revolves on its name
    Only

    In this land
    Phoebus Apollo will die hard
    This is the country of Sun

On oath to live forever
Of what use is a tie-and-die of heroes
(We crucified)
On our walls against his force?
Or why try to electrocute him with an
Iamb of electricity per week?
No need to call him to Yamoussoukro
Or make Clint Eastwood's bus in the Gauntlet
Of his Chariot
Phoebus Apollo dies hard

In this city
Phoebus Apollo will die hard
This is the city of Ra
Heliopolis
Hurray, hurrah
A ray and a rah
For the city
The legacy of a monstrance that
Mystified our minds to bend to
An unquenchable god
24 years ago
For 24 years

In this heritage
Phoebus Apollo will die hard
Phoebus Apollo has sworn to die hard
In this heritage of 24 years ago
For 24 years during which
Mammy Queens were
Mesmerized with poly-tricks to the
Obelisk of Ra

This is the heritage of their obscenity
The bloody seeds spurn

A foliage of harlotry that
Stands up with a
Majiji of cleansing like
Hackles on the geranium of a glabrous chicken
Fighting

In this people
Phoebus Apollo must die hard
This is a priesthood sold
24 years ago
For 24 years on a
Transubstantiation of a vermillion god
At an altar on which they were the
Victims of the sacrifice

Bush Doctor
Chant your ragga
Spin the airwaves with that
Song that sells like hot buns
  Let the Sun shi-i-i-i-ne
  It haffi shi-i-i-i-ne...
Sing sing sing on
You sing the religion of a heritage
Hurray hurrah
A ray and a rah
For the city of rah
The altar of rah
Ad infinitum....

March 29th
Amid clatter of
Ragga, place names, and Sundance
Taxis come and go
This one comes and scorches Moses away at full blast into Sun
Leaving his sweat

The labor of his poetry
Steaming in the gutter
Pulling the plug on my poem on
April Fool's Day

Firstrain

february fourth
firstrain falls like
last drops of
urination

no ablution
no invigoration
but this suffocating
intensity of earth's
body odor

armpit steam
savage with
sun's penetration of earth
assaults housewalls
undersweats faces
with halitosis of faeces
from bush conveniences

lips pout

to spit disgust to the
luminous buttocks
hunched like giant toads
over the flowering of flies

/

to barricade the nares
from the fulsome
breath-attack

/

to suck-teeth the
damned rain
dribbling like
leak from the
impotence of
the sky

Donkey Blues

(Voice of a Sierra Leonean Cart Pusher in the Gambia)

I rap forage razed
By my donkeywork
Yeah! Rap forage razed
By my donkeywork
In sand tethered to Sun in the Gambia
Rapping forage razed
By my donkeywork

I dance my tail to
Tunes of my torment
Ooh! Dance my tail to
Tunes of my torment
Thrum of flies groove my yaws in the Gambia
Dancing my tail to
Tunes of my torment

I stomp my hoofs bruised
By my slave shackles
Humph! Stomp my hoofs bruised
By my slave shackles
Lays of fleas pulse my hams in the Gambia
Stomping my hoofs bruised
By my slave shackles

I blow my bugle
Burst by my burdens
Yow! Blow my bugle
Burst by my burdens
In barbs of mangrove roots in the Gambia
Blowing my bugle
Burst by my burden

Sleepless in America

I dreamt sleep in the USA
To perch on the roadside
Where the blaze of Sundance
Has not consumed the corn

On the roadside
In the corn
The scheme of Sun
Is dance of sickle
In my eyes

Moon…Moon
That immemorial
Sycophant of Sun is
Fishhook in the flesh
Of my sleep

Sun jerks the hook
Sickle slashes skin
Down my spine
Tears sleep
From my dream

And I am forced to backslide
To tears

Back into the blaze of Sundance

Ibadan Revisited

With its own reckless hands
This conurbation has completely wrecked itself
The far-flung roofs of its slums rot with rust in bloodsucking sun

Along the cracked skulls of its carriageways, traffic is dead...
Festers beside carcasses of cars, trucks, trailers, tankers, tippers
Okadas killed by cutthroat mechanics

Only cacophony survives the collateral scrapping
Even Clark's glimmering seven hills have died under this
Crushing spread of man

New Dawn

They say Sun is now on a leash…. They say
Democracy yanks him back from yapping after dreams
Running scared through fields of scorched elephant grass

But (this poet sees) in the viewfinder of a seer's camera
Out again from the shadows of his ubiquitous scowl
The bloody-minded eyeball of Sky rises to hound

The vagabond hopes of those whose hunger
Fed the resurgence of his scepter

Power Tussle

Blow by blow
The saga offloads
Bales upon bales of dirty
Linens and tricks of
Machiavellian politics
Unfold

Who at the end of
These already
Worn out days of our lives
Gets the toga
Now pulled to bits and
Pieces in this
Fratricidal tug of war?

No water to clean
Clear the gathering questions

No questions to unravel the
Grime and fishy
Smell of familiar intentions

No questions answered
Until the oracle of history speaks

And time alone is
The ultimate truth teller

Powergrip

If the lichens must
Clutch on, their tendrils
Of power must suck
Up to the Kalashnikov

The experts in this
Deadly peacekeeper
Must feed fat on pols
To crack a common outcry

Funk in Freetown

Ears wake wide open as
Windows in the morning
Tiptoe as if late for Egugun dance
To snoop into Harmattan for news
Fresh as rumors of Rebel War

Emotions erupt into sweat like high noon
Beneath elephant heads of rebel ravages
Peace of minds lifts into flight like
Blinds at windows wide open to
Harmattan late in December

Hearts drop to floors as night fall
Funk in shadows of board windows and
Country-cloth curtains
Sleepless to cease the instant
Kalashnikovs crack Harmattan with
Sputters of Rebel Lion in town

Knock Iron Soja

Sankoh bails war
To Pujehun

Gun bales burst
For the experts

So soja sees
Soja sees time

To knock iron
When it is hot

With eyes red as
APC thug

Liver loaded
With gunpowder

Talking tough with
Boneheaded boots

He goes bursting
Bare peasant butts

Gov'ment Wharf rat
Turned soja now

Alligator
Pepper pyric

With gov'ment gun
To knock iron

He goes kicking
Life with left foot

Cracking his own
Calabashes

Sacking his own
Sacrifices

Burning the threads
Of his own shroud

Symbol/Eyes

(To Foday Sankoh)

This you no thin
Quarrel about nothing
Brother
Becomes desert under our feet
Barrels through the land
Guzzles our dream in
Kolanut's eye

In Kolanut's eye
The dream is
ONEBLOOD SPLITS THE PUMPKIN
The pumpkin, the conch that
Holds seeds of your
Dust devils in Needle's eye

In Needle's eye
Sandstones of your niggles stride
Devouring every space
Brother
Between already bloodied raw-sore toes
To the bone-marrow core of
Oneblood's eye

Darkness now. Chaos next
Blinded, Oneblood's eye
Scatters at the core
Becomes sandstorm in Needle's eye
A nightmare of running
Bloodbath in Kolanut's eye

And all these…
Deals of your psycho-palaver
Gone amok in
Bloodred eyes

Bo of THEPEOPLE

I am Bo
The Potter's Clay
Created to cradle
The prototype of
THEPEOPLE's indomitability

Those without my spirit
        THEPEOPLE is my spirit
Catch the dysentery of
Fear of death
At the blast of my name

I am Bo
The tigerroar of Poro
Giving birth to
THEPEOPLE's power in a
Sacred bush

None not of my spirit can touch
The private parts of my
Sacred labor and live
No not one invader can smell
The blood of my childbirth and
Live to tell it

THEPEOPLE is that labor
The birth pains of my productivity
The sweat of my sustenance
The blood of my self-sacrifice
To deliver my bloodline
From degenerates

Let degenerates come
O let the RUF come
With rough tactics
Let them come
With slaughter and despoliation
Let them come

Qaddafi trained
Taylor paid
Sankoh led
Real rebels
Renegades
Sobels
Let them all come

If truly truly
They know they weren't born with
A mother's curse on their heads
Let them come

If truly truly
They know they have
Testicles of a man like me
Let them come to meet me
Man to man

I draw a line in the land and
Dare them to cross it
I hold up two hands full of sand and
Dare them to bat one down

I am Bo
Their miry clay
The slippery soil to the waterhole which
Rivers of rebels and sobels cannot cross

THEPEOPLE is that waterhole
Open mouth of crocodile into which
Rebels and renegades dive
Body, soul, and spirit

Hear this and know
You who extol
     With pee of fear
     Trickling down your legs
Atrocities of the RUF

Go back to 1977
You who broadcast that
Life has been hacked in the face
With a machete

You who rumor that our mother's womb
Has been burst and dismembered with
RPGs and GPMGs

You whose aortas swell and explode
Heads and tails of the sun
Following a dark drama
Set-fired by the BBC

I say go back to history
You whose clay-pot of cool hearts
Has been kicked and burst open with
Iron-faced boots of RUF terror
History will let you know that

I am Bo
The Potter's Clay-pot
Worked with the heart of Kendekai

Bombs and bullets
Bounce off my cooked-rubber chest

I am Bo
The Potter's Clay-pot
Finished with the liver of Baba Yallah
Machetes and bayonets
Bend on the ironstone of my belly

I am Bo
The Potter's Clay-pot
Boiling with THEPEOPLE's
Stubborn will to live

When rebels, renegades and
Collaborators come killing and looting
THEPEOPLE will rise from the stepped-on tail
Of a black mamba

With one-bone strength of a baboon
THEPEOPLE will rise
To defend the black earth of
Our mother's nipples

And this generation
Will not pass away
Till the whole land sees
THEPEOPLE
Indomitable on the
Crocodile tail of
Self-determination

For Zainab Bangura
(10/2/96)

With the wild-weed
Spirit of elephant grass
You have ascended the
Sky of valiant flames

Mother of unsinkable calabashes
Defying our suffocations
In the rectums of big fishes

Just like our Jonah—
Singular sign of Poro pride in this
Machismo of suicidal murmurers—

You have ascended the
Sky of valiant flames to
Birth us one deathless moment

With the vigor of
Harvest rhythms that thump our
Villages on fullmoon nights

With the stoutness of
Stars that wear out the night &
Kiss the blue dazzle of new dawns

You have ascended the
Sky of valiant flames
To be crowned
Queen of our Renaissance

Grassroots Poet

(To Gbanabom Hallowell, for gathering us into FPS)

I am Falui
One-armed combustive poet
Twin brother of Elephant Grass

I who once stabbed my
Heart with torments for my Sierra
Shattered my grit on her
Peaks of pain

Now by the spirit of grassroots
Dance with bushfire &
Carry fury in memory of
Cobra smoked out of his hold

I uncoil my fangs into vibes
On the fire of all Sierra's rivers
To become a sea of poets
Skilled in rising from death

And I arise… I rise
Through the taproot tip of Cotton Tree
I emerge to surge through Sierra's bones
To purge forever from memory

The scandal of rapscallions
Turgid in the conch of
Her pubescence

BEATS IN PENUMBRA

Definition

Poets are
Poor eaters

Like this poem

Like this page

Nostalgia

Spirits passed and our village squares have come to utter silence

Mute now the music of the rice mortars of harvest days
When we weaved the hair of evening fires with deft dances
Drums, songs, and ululations evoked
The heartbeat of deepest desires
Laughter was life, profuse and pure as white clay of hope on
Bondo girls bantering about dream boys under a new moon
Their grass skirts suffused with susurrus of sweet innocence
Like boys and girls naked as peeled potatoes
Plunging into the pulse of August rain and not ashamed

Mornings would rise with flowers of weaverbirds choral in palm trees
Noons exult with the lyric eloquence of pepper
Birds praising their spice of life
Or blaze farm trails with panoplies of butterflies planting kisses
Across the breathing, fragrant, full-blown faces of petals
And we, barefooted, would climb the strong backs of breadfruit trees
Shake down to earth rumbles of their round bursting breasts
Drink the sun down from calabashes bubbly with god-to-man babble
Whistle to busty rhythms of maidens pounding boiled palm fruits as

Spirits passed, envious of our village squares settled to utter cadence

East of Eden

1/Adam

Man is stone
Prone to break and scatter
Unwilling to cleave
To roots, to flesh, to places

Man may mesmerize
For a moment
Hold like first kiss
Sizzle with animal heat

But stone is stone &
Man becomes stone
Turns cold and falls
Unable to rise

To cleave
To father
To lover
To mother-

Land

2/Eve

Gang-raped at twelve; the
Bloody child pushes to come—
Dilations of pain

3/Cain

Blood—
Voice box in the rifled
Throat of his brother
Hoarse with cries to God—
Aches in his head

Haunts him daily as
Zombies with hacked limbs
Howling for his head
In the ruined soul of
His homeland

Hunts him down daily
From the high hills of
His stoned crazy
Trigger-happy
Rebel days

4/Seth

In the name of God
He strikes the gong
Of his fierce tongue
Calling on God
　　　To fuel his combustive rage

In the name of God
With Book and sword
He drives his horde
Calling on God
　　　To goad his holy rampage

In the name of God
He kills and dies
Wills paradise
Calling on God
    To pile on his bloody wage

Invocation

Earth turned by the crush of the hungry
Earth turned by hands that blister at the
Dirty end of day

Tomorrow we come to revoke the prophecy of sorrow
Tomorrow we come to sow
May you

Heave to our dreams
Yield to our will
Open up when our seeds

Swell
Burst &
Dig to root in you....

Earth rich-dark as
Full moon of Areola
Nourishing round a thousand
Nursing nipples

Yield us dances on sheaves on our threshing floors
And measure our laughter in bushels

Monday

Morning crows along
Clumps of smoke
From firewood
Still wet with
Saturday's appetites

Sleep chokes coughs
Shakes with cold of
Seven-days rain
Wakes up yawning
To the atmosphere in
Fulaman bread

Out of bed
Life is dunked
Up and down
Like a teabag
Into a boiling
Rush for time

In the bathroom
The long-standing
Lack of tap water
Washes the face
From a soup bowl

And with pepper-water
In the eyes
Fingers grope into
Pockets for any yield
On last-and-last sweat
Sowed Sunday
On a pastor's plate

Sweat but no gain
Monday once again
Man steps into world again
To suck air
Under dog's umbrella
Hugging the hope of a
Cow with no tail

After...

After the Benz
And the power
And the purple
And the perfume
Dissipate

The Pa comes
Home to himSelf
For a night watch

His dry soul paces
The sleeping ceiling
The Grave question
Heavy upon his brow

Where Are You Now

How deep
To the depths
Have you
Sunk
Oh Foday
Sankoh

The stubborn
Lichens of your
Beard a
Scourge on your
Face
Heritage
Family
Your name

Shame holding the
Infernal black hole in
Your bloody
Backside—filled
With malodorous
Crap—to the
Full view of
The ages

The Legion that
Infested your
Always livid
Liver
Forever shreds
Off your
Skin
With iguana claws

As it drags down
Your hateful
Heartless
Soul
To battle demons
You birthed
In the bottomless
Pits of
Hell

Temptation

Drain your brain
Here, into my water closet

It is white
For identity
American Standard
For class

I see your image
Already in
With my excretions
Head over heels

Throw in your brain
Runaway African boy

Matter of course
It will not waste
This is the US
We recycle and reuse
First class

Of course
You should know
Your queens & princes
Once drained here

Give up brains bright-eyed boy
Come clean Mickey-D's toilets

Great Expectation

Gets yet another letter
From his brother

The one who washes plates
In the United States

Rips open the envelope
Of his last hope

For even a dollar
To lift the collar

Of his life lived too long
Yes, lived much too long

Like a tail stuck in the bog
Between the legs of a shamed dog

Complex
(Street Talk recorded)

The man's words came thick
As epileptic foam

think about blackout
you think about blackman
think about black lists
you think about blackman
think about black lies
you think about blackman
think of blackmarkets
you think about blackman
this black body no good....

His self-image caught me as
Doorhandle a Fulaman's gown
Rending my heart

when those people looked at us peeeeeeeeeeeeeengh
and called us monkeys
you think it was for nothing?
was it for nothing?
i tell you
we are like that
we cannot part with our black palms
we cannot part with our black ways....!

I stood under the barrage
More stunned than stone
Thinking
No wonder
With such a mind
It is no wonder

Brother
You hang behind like buttocks
To sit on.

Bo by Bus

The high charge
Dropped from the
Motorboys's
Lips like wet ash
No blood
No fire
No spirit

Just "three tawa"
And we knew
Better than to
Bend down to
Touch his feet
With our fingers

"Get inside"
He spoke as
To fowls

With our bags
And stuff
We got in
To be packed
Flesh upon flesh
Toe on toe
Bone to bone
Some squeezed
Like sardines
Against steel

Only
Here there was
No oil

No spittle
No swallowing

Just human beings
Hard
On each other.

Retired

Day
Flat out on its back
Like a *Raid*ed cockroach

Night
An anthology of dreams
Bookmarked by insomniac blues

On the sofa of a lover's palate
The air conditioner
Snores

A full-throated vexation along
The verges of mosquito
Wings

Ode to Storm

Thunder
Down rain

Thunder down
You spitting storm

Lash your mad machetes
At our stripped moments

Slant your slashes as savage cut-
Lasses cutting grasses

At the roots
Below the belt

As you rain down
Thunder

Epitaph

(Remembering my son who died at birth)

Your face
From the long distance
Of elephant's memory

Your face
Lazarus come forth
Smack out of my loins

Fair-skinned sesame
Seeds of your face
More fertile than death

Face with footprints—
As pregnant turtle's—
Beamed from beyond stars

Always lights a child's first
Smile of solace on my
Father face

Counterpoint

(In Memory of Ben Ecklu)

You have fired a first finger
Into the eyeballs of death
And have burned down the shiver
In the cold hold of its shadow and stare

So the old man
           The grave
                    With his boat
      Full of his own ashes
           Floats
          Adrift
                              Towards the edge
Where his infernal river falls off to drown in
Abyss

You have packed lavish laughter
Into life's lip-lock with loss,
Romanced a widow's drawn out dirge
To jazz and dance on the wing spans of Seraphs

So let now the low
           Doleful drum
       Beat of saints
               Shuffle & swing
        Lift a lilt
             While you
    Waltz a-
Cross rhythms to enter eternal supernal
Bliss

Twilight

Long drawn out days
We waiting, breathing in our pain
Holding our breath on thoughts of you…

You still gone
Still groveling under some
Paradise seeker's psychopathy...

God!

We praying, breathing out our hopes
Letting our dreams out into
Dark nights in search of you...

You still holding out
Like some unflinching lodestar
High up in the skies of paradise…

This Your Birthday

Is a far cry from home
Is a cry far from home
Is cry
Cry as howling house of
Sahelian storms where
Turmoil never blows over
Dust never settles
Bloodied tears

Smiles now lay in ruins
No elixir left in laughter
As if this day was born to explode
Shudder upon shudder
Like blasts from a double suicide
Mission in the best of memories.

O votary, soldier sworn to fight for forever fortunes
Have we this day crossed the crux toward Armageddon?
If so, cry too has teeth to goad desert storms
And cry is all there is left for the sea and its stolen children
So cry the sea will
Cry we all will
Cry is all till

Our brother &
The girls come back home

Feeling Free?

How does it feel
To sniff common air
To have a whiff of life
Free of manacles and
Clatter of suicidal tongues in
Acerbic accents?

How does it feel
To plunge deep into sleep
To dream dreams
Free of the Nightmare of buxom
Maidens tantalizing cutthroats to a
Godforsaken paradise?

How does it feel
To wear frisky feet like Nafali
To skip and scamper
Free with the effervescence of raffia flames
No longer dispossessed of your
Spirit to dance?

How does it feel
To come home to me brother
To convoke, like a durbar, a
Free flow of tears from familial felicities
Our intoxicated, praise-singing mother
Ululant for your freedom at last?

How does free feel?

For Khadi

(Mark 5:24-31)

Nefertiti, is it your body
Like the half moon
Half drained of nerve and verve
Half in a ray of faith and hope
I see shoved around
By a crush of whispers?

Hold heart
Soul sister of the fertile
Long-lived Nile
Alas, the tongues of alter egos
Do cackle with tattle
Gossips run in the genes of wet markets

The back-turned feet of little people
Walk their little minds
To sit on little benches
For small talk
In the backyards of their
Small towns

But trust you
Even as one side of you staggers
Under darkness of pain and betrayal
The bright side of you
Will not let their back bites
And their back stabs
Assail your reach towards just
One touch of God

Stich by stich
Along the hem of a miracle
The half-moon will come to fullness
With full-throated songs of poetry
Every fiber of your reborn face
Fully threaded with the silk
Strength of virtue
From the Word
Lord of rejuvenescence

Ubuntu

Life is
Lived not in time and season
Not in the tick
Tock of the clock
That winds down to broken
Balance wheels or dead
Batteries to be
Chucked in a bin for
Reincarnation

Life is
Lived on and on
Within the endless
Circles of inseparable arms that
Surround the baobab tree
With firm embrace of
Family
Friends
Mates
Strangers on the road that bind
I to 1

Integrity within integer
Regardless the diversity of
Dreams
Aspirations
Color or creed
The zillion ways each falls and is raised
To kindle this single space shared
Within each

Life is
Lived best where Africa

Once got it
In its philosophy of
Paradise as community
Where nONE is
Good enough to be alONE
Where nONE is
God enough to be
I AM.

Goombay for Kainwo

Out of the bulls
Eye of the bush
Buffalo's heart
Land, drum
Beats burst—
A blaze.

Some awe
Some, awe-inspiring
Phenomenon of taut
Talking tom
Toms
Aboil with hot iron
Tongues of fire—

Forest deep
Vocables of a sac
Red, bearded
Bard with indelible
Oracles on the back
Side of his face—

Alights with dazzling
Cadence & dance
Like izzards of
Unquenchable thunderbolts
On the tympanum of our
Nation in the doldrums

Kicks in a quick
Tick into our toes
Zippy up the
Pelvis to our back

Bones & then
Breaks
Out of our bone
Marrows with one
Cracking carnival

Across the country

GLOSSARY

3 Days, 7 Days, 40 Days: Ceremonial funeral days in Sierra Leone.

APC: All Peoples' Congress, a dominant political party in Sierra Leone.

Arata: Krio for 'rat'

A tink say san do dem: I think sun bewitched them.

Big Sissy: Literally, 'big sister' but also refers to a woman living the highlife.

Bintumani: A popular and prestigious beachside hotel in Freetown named after the highest peak in Sierra Leone.

Bo is the main commercial and administrative hub of Southern Sierra Leone, and the country's second largest city.

Bondo (also known as Sande) is the exclusive female secret society in Sierra Leone where adolescent girls go through the traditional rites of passage to become adults.

Coocoo: A Mende game of hide-and-seek.

Egugun: A Krio masquerade

En you ge de voice: And you have the voice.

Foday Sankoh was the founder and leader of the Revolutionary United Front (RUF), which waged an atrocious 10-year civil war in Sierra Leone from 1992. Sankoh received his guerilla training in Qaddafi's Libya and took his marching orders from Charles Taylor, who himself launched a devastating rebel war in neighboring Liberia in 1989.

Foofoo (or fufu) is a Sierra Leonean dish made from fermented cassava, and served in balls.

Falui is a one- armed masker feared for its "whip of discipline," but also loved for its entertaining dance and classical Mende oratory. FPS refers to the Falui Poetry Society, a group of young Sierra Leonean writers who came together in the early years of the civil war to hone their craft and establish a vigorous literary culture in the country.

Fula: A largely immigrant group from Guinea renowned for their bread-baking and neighborhood shops.

Gambe: Name for the Gambia in Sierra Leone.

Goombay (also Gumbe) is a genre of music from Freetown, characterized by acoustic sound and pulsating rhythms on locally made drums and other percussive instruments

Government Wharf: A landmark jetty in Freetown around which is a fishing community, infamous for street urchins

Heliopolis: City of the sun.

Kendekai and **Baba Yallah** gained legendary status during the 1977 civil unrests in Sierra Leone. It is claimed that they were impregnable to man-made weapons and so were able to defeat truckloads of the Internal Security Unit (ISU) dispatched by the then President, Siaka Stevens, to put down protests against his government in Bo and other key towns around the country.

Jonah refers to Dr. James Jonah, a chief advocate for democracy in Sierra Leone during the 1990s

Limba: an ethnic group in Sierra Leone known for performing vigorous dance routines.

Lucky Dube: A popular reggae artist in Sierra Leone.

Majiji: Excessive body movement, intended to impress.

Mammy Queen: A high society woman, usually with political influence.

Nafali is a Mende masquerade reputed for its sprightly and masterly dance steps

Okomfe Anokye's sword is firmly stuck in the ground in Kumasi, Ghana. Okomfo Anokye is the legendary priest said to have received the sword from the Asante god. It is believed that the sword can never be removed from its place.

Phoebus Apollo: Ancient Greek sun-god.

Poro is the most powerful and dominant male secret society in Sierra Leone.

Pujehun: Due to its proximity to Liberia, Pujehun District in Southern

Sierra Leone was one of the first areas attacked when the RUF launched their armed rebellion.

Ra: Ancient Egyptian sun-god.

Ragga: Short for 'raggamuffin', a fusion of Jamaican reggae with American hip-hop.

Rapel: An ample shirt worn by men, typically with embroidery around the neck.

Sangba: A Mende tom-tom made of goatskin stretched over its hollow top.

Setfire: To deviously incite a fight

Sobel: During the Sierra Leone civil war, a government soldier who operated very much like am RUF rebel, meting out atrocities on the people he was supposed to protect.

Shegita: In Hunting Secret Society, the language of the dead or ancestral spirits.

Tawa: Krio slang for 'thousand'

Titi Bum Boat: The term bum boat (also bamboat or bambote) may have been coined in reference to prostitutes who frequented trade and supply boats from overseas, during the early days of Krio settlement in Freetown. The term is now generally used for any promiscuous person. Titi means 'girl'.

Undersweat: A kind of chokehold in local wrestling.

ACKNOWLEDGEMENTS

I am deeply grateful to the editors and publishers of newspapers, journals, and anthologies where versions of some of the poems in this collection first appeared:

- Dr. Julius Spencer of the *New Breed* newspaper in Sierra Leone was the first with the courage to outdoor any of the poems, including "Titi Bum Boat."
- "Sleepless in America," "On Setripe Sex," "Funk in Freetown," "We Light Our Fires in The Village," "Awaking Just Before Dawn," and "Sung for Jonah" first appeared in different volumes of *100 Words*.
- The People's Educational Association of Sierra Leone (PEA) first anthologized "Bo by Bus," "Lust," Gambe River Gal," "No Beautiful Woman," "After," and "Legs and Dreams" in *Lice in the Lion's Mane: Poets and Poems from Sierra Leone*, edited by Hannah Hope Wells.
- "Donkey Blues," "Casanova," "Titi Bum Boat Is a Towel," "Freetown from New England Ville," "Sugar Daddy Dance," "Complex," "A Tink Say San Do Dem," and "En You Ge De Voice" first appeared in *The Iowa Review*.
- Mohamed Gibril Sesay and Moses Kainwo first published "Great Expectation," "The Plague Advances," "Your Love Scares Me," and "Sexual Egotism Repulsed" in the anthology *Songs that Pour the Heart*.
- Kirsten Rian included "Bo of the People," "Knock Iron Soja," "Nostalgia," and "Solar Songs" in *Kalashnikov in the Sun: An Anthology of Sierra Leonean Poets*.
- "Ibadan Revisited," "Epitaph," "Counterpoint," and "Grassroots Poet" made their first appearance in *Leoneathology*, edited by Gbanabom Hallowell.

The poems in this collection would probably never have been published if not for the encouragement and support of the following special people in my life, to whom I owe depths of gratitude:

- Fellow writers Oumar Farouk Sesay, Mohammed Gibril-Sesay, Moses Kainwo, and Elvis Gbanabom Hallowell who have been brothers beyond Falui Poetry Society—that mystical collective which cut our teeth as writers.

- My wife, Bridget Maama, once threatened to bury me with my poems if I did not publish them, and has remained an ardent enthusiast despite my self-doubts.
- Carolyn Brown took breaks out of the stress of attending to her sick mother to provide editorial advice.
- Sheikh Umarr Kamara, Rowena Torrevillas, Joanna Skelt, and Glory Odemene read the manuscript and provided lavish encouragement and praise.
- Professor Frederick Woodard, Marc Nieson, and my colleague John Reaume have in one way or the other provided emotional support through the years.

www.ingramcontent.com/pod-product-compliance
Lightning Source LLC
LaVergne TN
LVHW011400080426
835511LV00005B/356